Careers in Sports

Also by Bob and Marquita McGonagle

Careers in Aviation in the Sky and on the Ground
Prepare for a Career in Radio and Television Announcing

Careers in Sports

Bob and Marquita McGonagle

Illustrated with photographs

Lothrop, Lee & Shepard Company
A Division of William Morrow & Company, Inc.

New York

In loving memory of our parents
James and Elizabeth McGonagle and
George and Anna Olsen

4   5
Library of Congress Cataloging in Publication Data
McGonagle, Bob.
    Careers in sports.
    SUMMARY: Surveys the wide variety of jobs in professional sports, in-
cluding those of administrators, managers, coaches, trainers, players, sports-
casters, and many more.
    1. Professional sports—Juvenile literature.
[1. Sports—Vocational guidance.   2. Vocational guidance]   I. McGonagle,
Marquita, joint author.
II. Title.
GV734.M3   796'.023   75-14460
ISBN 0-688-41709-4
ISBN 0-688-51709-0 lib. bdg.

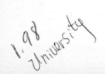

Careers in Sports

Contents

Many of us spend much of our leisure time and money watching sports events at huge stadiums such as this one. COURTESY NEW YORK METS

1 / Sports,
Where the Money is

Whether you watch or participate in them, sports can be fun. No wonder earning a living in athletics seems an ideal way to spend one's working life. If this type of career appeals to you, this book will help you select a realistic goal and tell you the best way to go about reaching it.

Notice that the word "realistic" is used. Many young people think of a career in sports as a playing career. But it is not realistic to expect that more than a comparative few will ever become the "professional athlete." But as you will see, the field is so wide a sports career need not be closed to the non-athlete. Even a hurried glance at the sports scene will show you people in top positions—club presidents, teachers, sportscasters, and others mentioned in this book—who never even earned a letter in high school sports. High school gym may have been a "hard subject." But they all have one thing in common with the athletes— a love of the sport, and a deep interest in all its angles.

The door to a sports career is never closed to the person who shares that feeling, not if you're willing to work hard, long hours, and swallow your share of disappointments.

If that sounds like the formula for success in many another career, it is.

What are sports?

Sports can be defined in many ways. They are sometimes games of competition where physical skills and body movement make them different from other kinds of games such as checkers or Monopoly. Sports may also be a non-competitive, though physical form of recreation, such as mountain climbing or fishing.

Sports can also be looked upon as an extension of play. Babies play in the simplest manner, perhaps rolling a ball. Children play in a more organized fashion, that is, with rules and time limits, such as in hopscotch. Sports are highly structured. In other words, you're at play dribbling a basketball in your own backyard. When you're dribbling a basketball in a school game, you're taking part in sports.

Sports may take place within the physical education department in schools, but not all physical education is sports.

Sports can also be show business and entertainment. Many events are handled and promoted in much the same way as a Broadway show. Can you find a better example of entertainment than the performances of the Harlem Globetrotters?

Some sports are considered "art." An example of this is an ice skating event. Many people see skating in much the same way as they do ballet.

Sports reach into international politics, too. Look at the way table tennis has served as a bridge between China and the United States.

National policies are sometimes affected by sports, as in the case of countries that lift "color" or race barriers to permit participation by their athletes in international competition.

City leaders plan for sports areas and arenas and budget huge sums of money for convenient means of transportation and roadways to reach them. They know that if they neglect such programs they may have to look for another job after the next election.

However we look at sports, most of us spend much of our leisure time and money either taking active part in them or watching others participating in them. This has made sports a multi-billion dollar industry. And it is still growing—a fact that adds up to more job opportunities for you.

The big money

Within the last few years, interest in sports in this country has grown at a feverish pitch. Big leagues add more divisions or teams. The playing season lengthens like the line at the stadium's box office. The cost of tickets rise, along with the salaries of the players.

Stadiums cost $50 million or more to build. New franchises (teams) in the hockey league that cost $2 million apiece just a few years ago are now priced at over $6 million.

Tax dollars paid yearly by racetracks to state governments have climbed to over the half-billion mark.

Sports equipment, goods, and clothing amount to about 50 billion dollars in sales each year.

The television marriage

Today almost every professional sport is controlled in some strong way by the television networks. It is television money (totaling more than $150 million each year) that causes the referee to call "time out" when the director signals it's time for a "message from our sponsor." Television networks, in turn, may receive over $200,000 for a one-minute commercial broadcast during a big sports event.

Schedules are often set for the best television viewing time, but the team owners and players don't seem to mind. Television coverage of a sporting event often introduces the contest to people who have never seen it before and encourages them to spend money to see the event in person.

Television earnings mean there's more money available for players' salaries. And a portion of that income also goes into the players' retirement funds. TV money means more work and income for many non-players, too.

Sports and television representatives may battle over many issues in public and in private. The union is not always a happy one. But the bond shows no sign of weakening, for it would be impossible for either to exist as profitably without the other. And, as in other businesses, profit is the name of the game.

13

2 / The Athletes

Rooting for a player or for the entire home team will set our hearts pounding. But participating, not watching, usually has the greatest appeal in sports, whether it's tag or baseball, bobsledding, or jumping over a fence astride a horse.

When we play, we strive to be the best. If we lose, we congratulate the winner, and hope we'll get the pat on the back the next time around. A tie is never satisfactory to either the player or spectator.

All that glitters

A young athlete with talent learns early that he or she is set apart from other people. The blue ribbon won for the fifty-yard dash in grade school gives a little-known student a taste of attention. An important touchdown scored in a high school or college football game showers the player with respect and popularity. And those whose special skills have earned them the title of "professional athlete" often find rewards greater perhaps than do those in many other

14

Professional athletes are the folk heroes of our time. Fans seek their autographs. COURTESY NEW YORK METS

professions. A professional athlete is someone who participates in a sport for money, for prizes such as cars and television sets, as well as for glory.

About 36,000 professional athletes in the United States compete in individual sports such as tennis or golf or in team sports such as basketball. What is their biggest reward? Many would probably answer "money." And for those who reach the top, that answer could be a right one. Salaries for playing in the big time top those of most presidents and prime ministers.

Professional athletes may also sweeten their pocketbooks with money earned from being on television programs and making public appearances. By endorsing certain products, that is, announcing that they wear a special brand of shoe or eat a certain kind of food, athletes may also add greatly to their bank accounts. Some write books or magazine articles (or permit their name to be used as the author). Others appear in motion pictures, or on the stages of Broadway, or in glittery Las Vegas hotel shows.

There are other advantages, too. The professional athlete is the folk hero of our time. Playing professionally, even for a few months, adds a dimension—a "star" quality —to his or her reputation and character that may last a lifetime.

The sorry side

There are disadvantages to a professional athletic career as well. One is that the playing life of most athletes lasts only a few years. This means that their main occupation will most likely be something else. And that "something else" usually does not begin until their playing days are over. Others in that same career will have had a big headstart at the job.

Travel! See the country . . . the world! Most professional athletes consider travel an advantage only until the novelty wears off. Then it comes to mean a lonely time away from the family. They must adjust to changes in time and climate. And the meals and beds never seem as inviting as at home.

16

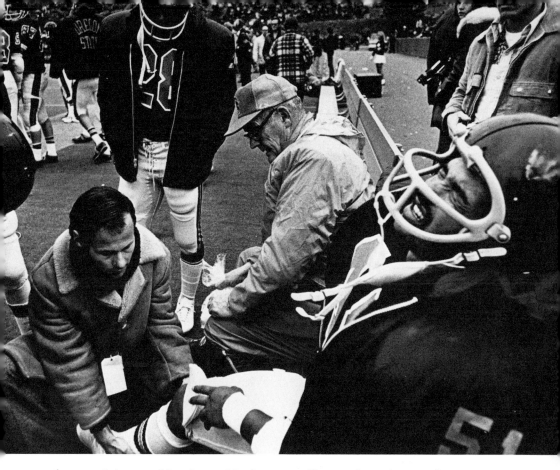

A severe injury could end an athlete's career. Here a player is treated by a team physician. COURTESY OF ALBANY DEMOCRAT-HERALD. ALBANY, OREGON

Another minus—athletes seldom get to choose the location in which they wish to work. Most other people do.

Also, the athlete always faces the possibility of a severe injury that could mark an early end to his or her career. If the injury happens while the athlete is playing for a big-team club, like those mentioned in the next chapter, the club is obligated to pay the salary for the rest of that contract year, but no longer. Of course some clubs do feel that helping the injured player is the right thing to do and will continue doing so even after the contract has ended.

Competition keen

Despite the drawbacks, the gold and glamour offered the professional athlete provide enough attraction to make the race for jobs as competitive as an Olympic track event.

Holding on to the job can be just as hard. Even if the athlete has been around a long time and has a fine record, he or she sees young, capable people waiting to step in at the first sign of slowing down or weakening.

Requirements

Each sport requires certain special abilities and standards of its athletes. But every sport shares certain requirements in common. One is that the athletes must be in top physical condition. They must also want to play and to win—to become a champion! They need also to love the game or sport enough to put up with the demands of grueling work, constant practice, and sometimes hardships.

The best players have some, perhaps most, of the following characteristics: speed, muscular coordination, excellent eyesight, determination, endurance, quick reflexes, confidence, and the weight and height correct for a particular sport or game.

Professional athletics demand a high level of mental and emotional performance, too. And if you get along with others, that's also an asset, especially for team sports.

Education

More and more athletes are becoming well-schooled. More than half have college educations. (Very often the only road to a playing career winds through a college campus.) Athletes major in college in everything from language arts

Most schools today have extensive sports programs. Students in this picture wait to take to the field. COURTESY CENTRAL JUNIOR HIGH SCHOOL. GREENWICH, CONN.

to political science and when their playing days are over may enter a field entirely unrelated to sports.

But most go into sports because they love it and would not be happy in another career area. Luckily for them, by working at the sport, or training in it, they have gained special skills that can be put to new use. Some become referees or coaches, others sell sporting goods or teach. These and other non-playing careers are discussed in other parts of this book.

19

The military services have many sports and athletic programs. The outstanding athletes are encouraged to enter international competition. COURTESY U.S. NAVY

The road to professionalism

Most schools today have extensive physical education and sports programs. Outstanding high school athletes are often offered college scholarships. And success in college sports will almost certainly result in an invitation for the athlete to work at the sport professionally.

The military services have sports and athletic programs,

too, with training and clinics available for improving techniques. Trials and contests bring to the surface the best athletes.

Many are selected from the military, schools, colleges, and from private areas for international competition. They might enter, for example, the Pan American Games, or the Olympics. Being a winner in any large contest, especially the Olympics, opens many doors. The main reason, of course, is that a winner is one of the very best athletes in the world. Another reason is that an Olympic medal winner becomes an instant celebrity. Owners and managers of sports teams know that such an athlete on the team roster or performing with a group (such as an ice skating show) will help draw spectators. Corporations are more interested in sponsoring programs that feature such an athlete, too.

Your future as a pro athlete

If you are a talented, young athlete, should you be encouraged to aim for a professional career? If that's what you really yearn to do, the answer must be yes. But do so with the knowledge that only a few of the thousands and thousands of young people who try will make it. For that reason, it is important that you ready yourself for another means of earning a living should you fail to make the player's roll call.

And since a playing career is often finished in a few years, you should also look ahead to when you will be thirty or forty. What would you like to do with your life then?

3 / The Big Team Players

Only a few people will make it to the major leagues of football, baseball, basketball, hockey, and soccer. But you should know how these teams operate and how the players live, for in the next chapter you'll find out about the many jobs and careers that lie behind the scenes of the playing field. And all of those jobs revolve about the players and team.

Baseball

About 3,000 professional athletes earn a living playing baseball. You could probably name most of the major league teams and many of the players. But not so with the minor leagues. They are filled mostly with young and unknown hopefuls. The question always uppermost in their minds is, "Will I be drafted by a major league team?" The hope that they will inspires them to work and practice for little money while traveling from one small town to another for games.

Sometimes older players who are no longer able to meet the requirements of the big leagues, drop to the minors

About 3,000 professional athletes earn a living playing baseball.
COURTESY NEW YORK YANKEES

and play there for a few years before retiring completely.

Baseball players usually begin their professional careers at a very young age. They are discovered playing in high school and college or on sandlot teams. If selected by a scout, they begin by playing in the minor leagues, although a few go right to the majors. Most never make it out of the minors.

Spring training heralds the start of the baseball season in February or March, in warm, southern climates.

The schedule during the season is a tough one. Teams play one and sometimes two games a day—half the games at their home stadium and half at their competitors' fields. There is seldom more than one free day between a series of games and that day is often spent traveling.

During the off season, these athletes are expected to keep themselves physically fit. Some do so by playing with teams outside of the United States.

Minor league players often earn below $5,000 a year. Major league players start at about $15,000 and earn up to $150,000 or more annually, but the average salary is about $37,000.

Football

Almost all the pro football players come from college teams. A few make it by playing in the military service or in minor league football. But even those teams get most of their players from colleges.

The average salary is about $27,000 a year. First year players earn about $23,000. Some top stars earn $150,000 or more. Not bad for about six months work!

Players report to training camps in the middle of July for classroom lectures and practice sessions. As the days go by, the training grows more severe with scrimmage and heavy body contact with the other players. During the last several weeks of training, they play about one game a week with other teams. During this time, some players

The average playing life of a professional football player is less than five years, so new team members are constantly replacing older ones.
COURTESY NEW YORK FOOTBALL GIANTS

have to be dropped to keep the team within the number allowed by National Football League rules. Teams in other sports must do the same.

Players are subject to injuries during practice, exhibition, and regular games. They play in weather that may be hot and humid, or freezing cold. Snow, sleet, or rain may turn the field into a sea of mud.

There are over two dozen major football teams in the

25

United States. They employ over a thousand players. But the average playing life is less than five years so new team members are constantly replacing older ones.

Basketball

Pro basketball players number about four hundred. Like football players, most are drafted from college. Business organizations also sponsor teams and sometimes scouts find talented players there.

The pro career of a basketball player lasts only about seven years. The turnover creates a few openings each year.

Salaries in the National Basketball Association average about $90,000 a year. First year players may earn $18,000 or more, and some are in the $100,000 or more bracket. All this for playing a game they love on large, modern courts that are indoors and climate-controlled!

Basketball training season starts in October. The playing season starts in November and continues into May.

Most players are well over six feet tall. But a few shorter people who are exceptionally fast and capable have found a home with a major team.

Hockey

Over 800 professional hockey players work in this country and in Canada. Most professionals start in one of the several minor leagues, rise after two or three years to the majors, and then may return to the minors until their playing days are over.

Fall training starts in September. The playing season begins in October and ends in May. The professionals work out daily, even during the playing season.

Most basketball players are well over six feet tall. But a few shorter people who are exceptionally fast and capable have found work with a major league team. COURTESY ABC SPORTS

Well over 90% of the pro hockey players come from the cold climates of Canada and started to play this fastest of all games almost as soon as they learned to skate. But the quality of players in this country is improving because the

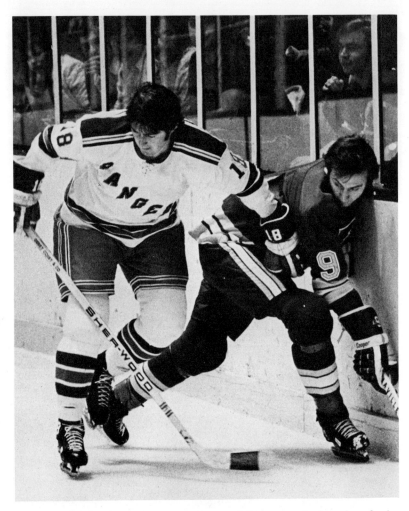

Professional hockey players work out daily, even during the playing seasons. COURTESY NEW YORK RANGERS

large number of year-round ice-skating rinks recently built or in the planning stage permit the same kind of practice opportunities that nature provides in lands farther north. Already in this country more than 250,000 Amateur Hockey League Association members now compete in a sport that has suddenly caught the public's fancy.

Summer hockey schools, too, number over 75, and permit enrollment for those as young as six years.

The earnings of hockey players have skyrocketed in recent years. The average National Hockey League player earns about $40,000 a year.

Soccer

In the five years from 1970 to 1975, the North American Soccer League grew from five to nineteen teams. Each year over a million spectators attend the games. But this is only a fraction of the number attending the other games mentioned. Pro football, for example, claims over 15 million paid admissions and major league baseball over 30 million.

In 1975 the League started the first indoor season (January through March). The comfort of indoor viewing should increase the number of spectators. Soccer is played outdoors from April until the end of August.

Most pro soccer players come from abroad, where the game has been popular for many years. Playing with such experienced players gives the American team members an opportunity to improve their performance. The League hopes that as the popularity of the game increases, more young American players will be good enough to make the pro teams. Salaries range from $700 a month for the less experienced players to $1000 a month or more for those at the top of the sport.

Only recently have soccer games begun to be televised. And as that happens, if this sport follows the pattern of others, its popularity will grow. So will the number of careers and jobs associated with soccer and the money to pay for them.

29

Soccer is a fast growing sport in America. COURTESY NEW YORK COSMOS

The big prize

The salary of the big team player is only part of the prize. Almost all sports leagues have set up "deferred payment plans." This means simply that a part of the huge salary is held out for a payment to the athlete when the playing days are over and the salary drops to zero.

Generous retirement plans have been set up, too. But for many, the jackpot is the bonus received for signing a contract. For example, when one rookie put his name to a five-year basketball contract worth nearly a million dollars, he received the following: a $50,000 cash bonus, three luxury cars to be delivered over the five year period, and $2,000 a year to help pay for his housing. The player's mother was also hired to work for the club at a good salary.

One hockey league superstar was given a million dollar bonus for staying with the team.

Of course all the other benefits mentioned in Chapter 2 that go to professional athletes apply to the team members.

The draft

To keep the big teams as nearly even as possible in the level of performance, a system called the draft has been devised. This is the way it works. Names of top college players who are graduating and want to turn pro are listed. Team representatives meet for a few days, usually in New York, to select the players they wish from this list. The team that placed last in the standings that year, gets first choice. The team next lowest in the standings gets the next choice, and so on. Naturally the representative will select the player the team needs the most.

If one team gets a player that another team wants, that other team may trade an established team member or members for the draft choice. Naturally, a lot of wheeling and dealing goes on at this time.

College players are not supposed to accept any offers until graduation, nor are offers supposed to be made, but players and representatives have been known to make deals secretly.

Turning pro

When the athlete decides to sign with a team, whatever the sport, he or she is likely to be considered a "profit maker" by the team owners. Like other business people, owners are interested in keeping costs down. Athletes should consider hiring a representative to help them gain the best possible financial position. Such agents should be highly respected and trained business people, not yes-men who promise pots of gold. Other advantages and disadvantages should be thought over carefully and discussed with experts. Only after a thorough consideration of terms should a contract be signed.

4 / The Team Behind the Team

When we watch a sports event, we seldom think of all the people behind the scenes who help make it possible.

On the professional level, administration is probably the single area in sports that offers the most opportunity for employment. This area divides into two categories. One contains the executive departments that oversee sports, such as the office of the baseball commissioner and the National Collegiate Athletic Association. These groups are concerned with rules and regulations and employ staffs ranging from public relations people to attorneys.

But the administrative departments that offer the most employment are the managements of the teams themselves. Baseball teams have the largest such organizations. Other sports have similar departments and, with some variation, the same kinds of job opportunities. But because of its long-established structure, let's use baseball as an example.

The owners

It takes a lot of money to buy a ball club. The purchaser must have a few million dollars to invest or know how to

33

get the financial backing for the purchase. Sometimes several people pool their money for the cause. Once a club has been purchased, the owners may leave the running of it to others, but some work hard as part of its managing team.

The best background you could have for this position is to be born very, very rich!

The general manager

The owner's first order of business is to find the best possible general manager. This person supervises the entire baseball operation, including hiring and firing, except for the actual direction of the games. The owner may take the bows like a king or queen, but the general manager is the ruling prime minister.

This person, of course, knows the sport thoroughly, and has a keen business and management sense. An education that emphasizes economics would help here.

The secretary

There is also a secretary—a lawyer who represents the club in legal matters. The department he or she heads writes up contracts, for example, not just with the players but with many others as well. A ball club does business with many people and organizations such as renters of space at the stadium, city agencies (the police, for example, regarding security or traffic at the stadium), and the sellers of equipment.

A law degree is necessary for any top position in this department. Law students may sometimes get jobs helping out during summer vacations.

This couple working on a project in the public relations department are husband and wife. COURTESY NEW YORK RANGERS

Public relations director

The public relations (PR) department is the funnel through which information about the club reaches the press, television, and radio and from them to us, the public. The director and other PR people try to get the club and players as much favorable publicity as possible. When you see a player signing a contract on a television news program, for example, you can be sure that a PR person made the arrangements.

Building public goodwill, not just getting the club's name

in the paper, is important, too. The men and women in this department place news stories, oversee club publications, reply to letters of criticism, arrange press conferences, and supervise activities in the press box. None of this is done in a casual way, but instead is a carefully planned and executed program.

Many colleges offer majors in public relations. Others offer courses in that field. A major in liberal arts provides a solid background for this work also.

High school courses in writing, journalism, public speaking, typing, and art could prove helpful. So would those that increase your understanding of human nature, such as psychology and history.

If a future in this field interests you, work now on your school paper and yearbook. Handle publicity for different school projects and programs. All this will help train you to take your creative ideas and put them to work.

The same kind of training and experience is advised for the next career field mentioned.

Promotion director

It's Bat Day, and a few thousand more families than usual show up at the stadium with their youngsters, who will be given inexpensive bats as they go through the admission gate.

Banner Day, and thousands of fans line up on the field to parade with banners created out of old bedsheets or cardboard, each with a message announcing in one way or another their devotion to the team or a favorite player.

Programs such as these, designed to increase attendance, are the brainchildren of the people in the promotion de-

Special events such as "Banner Day" are designed to increase atten-dance at the ball game. COURTESY NEW YORK METS

partment. They work closely with the public relations de-partment and are sometimes a part of it.

These employees are creative and imaginative. They must also be practical enough to be able to carry out their ideas once they are accepted by the promotion director.

Occasionally an exceptionally creative person uses his or her own abilities to work into this well-paying position without much formal education. But most people who rise in this department have a college education.

Another special public relations event is "Players' Family Day."
COURTESY NEW YORK METS

The comptroller

The comptroller is an accountant who directs financial matters for the organization. This person handles tickets, and monies received for other things, too, such as television rights and concession stands.

Bookkeepers, tax accountants, and other office people work under the comptroller.

If you would like a job in this department, plan now for a career in finance. All economic courses would be helpful; so would a legal background.

The traveling secretary

The traveling secretary arranges the travel plans for the

athletes and those who travel with them. This job requires getting the players, journalists, publicity people and all the other behind-the-scenes people in and out of the cities where the event is taking place. He or she also sees to the living and food accommodations, and anything else that may be needed on an out-of-town trip. Trying to satisfy everybody's taste in food, lodgings, and style of travel makes this job a particularly frustrating one. The ability to get along with people and skill at smoothing ruffled feathers is very important.

The person with a business education who handles details easily fits in nicely here. Experience with a travel firm, perhaps arranging tours, would also be excellent training.

The statistician

You hear an announcer say, "This is Joe's second longest hitting streak since he began playing baseball with the Giants in May of 1972." Facts and figures continue to roll easily off the announcer's tongue. He or she seems to be ad libbing, that is, speaking without a script. But the figures came from another club employee, the statistician, who comes up quickly with a new batting average each time a player goes to bat. Other such details are at his fingertips (where a computer is often found) and the data changes as the game goes on.

At the end of the playing season, the statistician puts all the statistics together in a book for the press. But the data isn't collected simply to satisfy curiosity. It's used to help determine how much the players are worth when contract-signing time rolls around.

An education in mathematics is what's needed in this job. Understanding the computer sciences helps, too.

The farm director

Each big league baseball club has a farm team or teams, part of the minor league system. It is there that promising ballplayers get the chance to show their stuff. And it's there that major teams look first for new talent.

The farm director, who oversees that operation, acts as go-between for the big club and the farm club. The farm director also sees to the scouting and sometimes to the signing of players' contracts.

The scout director

The scout director works with the scouts in the selection of the players they hope will move up the ladder to the big league. A ball club may employ many scouts, and the director sees to the activities of all of them.

Scouts

The constant search for new and better players has resulted in many full-time jobs as scouts. At one time the teams depended on friends to pass along the word about "a good little athlete I saw playing for a high school team in Boise." But scouting has now become a skilled job. It usually, but not necessarily, goes to former players whose experience is a plus for the job.

Scouts travel throughout the United States, and more and more often to other countries as well, searching for promising playing talent. Once they find the right person, they may sign the player on the spot. More often, though, there is considerable discussion and often legal advice is called for on both sides.

40

Getting on first base

These sports administration careers usually pay very well at the top, especially when they are associated with the large, wealthy organizations. The pay scale decreases with the size of the club and the amount of money it brings in. Many assistants and huge office staffs are often necessary. This area offers beginners the most realistic opportunity for employment. But jobs here are not easy to find, since they are highly prized by those waiting to get a foot in the door.

In administration, as in most sports careers, there is no one road to success. Many who made it were players at one time or another. Some were successful, some flopped. Others got their start in one area, and moved into another before starting to climb to the top.

Once in awhile someone gets a start by having a friend who is already in sports administration. The friend brings the job and the worker together. But the era of "who you know" and "luck" serving as wedges into such a career is coming to an end. There's too much money involved.

A few got their first job by answering an ad in the "help wanted" section of a newspaper. Others believed that their backgrounds and interests would qualify them for the job and started making the rounds. They visited personnel offices and filled out an application for employment. Others wrote letters to all the clubs asking for an interview. It is likely that most such letters are filed away with dozens of others. Yet there is always the possibility that yours will reach the right person's desk at just the right time. It has happened.

Education

Education is the most likely key to turn the lock on this

career door. The more education the more likely the "lucky breaks" will come your way.

One university, St. John's in New York, now offers a degree in athletic administration. Courses the students take include such subjects as the History of Sports and the Reading and Interpretation of Legal Documents.

It's never too early to discuss your college plans with your guidance counselor if a career in sports administration appeals to you. Your athletic coach's advice can be valuable, too.

ST. JOHN'S UNIVERSITY
NEW YORK
ST. VINCENT'S COLLEGE

Bachelor of Science Degree—Athletic Administration

DEGREE REQUIREMENTS	CREDITS
Business Law 1001	3
Communication Arts 1014	3
Computer Science 1021	3
English Composition 1003, *or* 1005, 1006	6
English Literature Electives	6
Management 1001	3
Mathematics 1003	3
Philosophy 1011, 1012, 1013, or 1014	9
Psychology 1001, 1002	6
Science 1002	3
Speech 1002	3
Sociology 1001, 1002	6
[1] Theology 1002, 1003, 1004, *or* 1008 *or* 1010	9
Major Area	36
[2] Free Electives	27
	126

[1] Non-Catholics may substitute appropriate Theology courses.
[2] Free electives may be chosen from any St. Vincent's College course. The following are strongly suggested as appropriate:
      Communication Arts 1001, 1002, 1009, 1027, 1028
      Management 1003, 1004, 1005
      Criminal Justice 1005, 1023

Recommended Sequence of Courses (Checklist)

42

FRESHMAN YEAR

Fall Semester	Credits	Spring Semester	Credits
English 1003 *or* 1005	3	English 1006	3
Mathematics 1003 *or* 1005	3	Speech 1002	3
Theology 1002 *or*		Theology 1002 *or* Philosophy	3
Philosophy	3	Sociology 1002	3
Sociology 1001	3	Free Elective	3
Free Elective	3	Athletic Administration	
	15	1008	3
			18

SOPHOMORE YEAR

Fall Semester	Credits	Spring Semester	Credits
English Elective	3	English Elective	3
Theology 1003 *or*		Theology 1003 *or* Philosophy	3
Philosophy	3	Psychology 1002	3
Psychology 1001	3	Athletic Administration	
Management 1001	3	1002	3
Athletic Administration		Athletic Administration	
1001	3	1003	3
	15	Free Elective	3
			18

JUNIOR YEAR

Fall Semester	Credits	Spring Semester	Credits
Theology 1004	3	Free Elective	3
Business Law 1001	3	Free Elective	3
Athletic Administration		Athletic Administration	
1004	3	1005	3
Science 1002	3	Athletic Administration	
Free Elective	3	1007	6
	15		15

SENIOR YEAR

Fall Semester	Credits	Spring Semester	Credits
Athletic Administration		Athletic Administration	
1006	3	1009	3
Athletic Administration		Athletic Administration	
1010	3	1011	3
Computer Science 1021	3	Free Elective	3
Free Elective	3	Communication Arts 1014	3
Free Elective	3	Philosophy	3
	15		15

43

5 / The Coach

The crowd watches the athletic coach give the player a pat of encouragement. They see him or her shout or whisper words of instruction and advice. It seems a simple job, one that certainly isn't as important as playing, but it is. Think what confusion there would be without the coach!

There are over 100,000 athletic coaches employed in this country. They work on three levels—(1) public and private high schools, small colleges, and a few grade schools, (2) professional and big-time college competition, and (3) instructional coaching such as golf and tennis, at clubs. This last level is discussed in Chapter 7.

What the coach does

The coach's job is twofold. First he is an organizer. He or she must decide how much time should be used to get the players in condition; how much on practice games; and what portion should be allotted to developing skills and teamwork. Scheduling games and practice sessions is his or her duty, also.

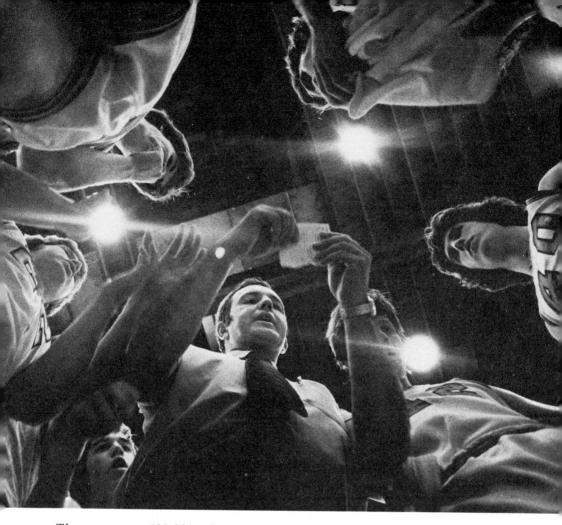

There are over 100,000 athletic coaches employed in this country. Here a high school coach gives last minute instructions to his team.
COURTESY OF ALBANY DEMOCRAT-HERALD. ALBANY, OREGON

In the larger schools a coach may specialize in one sport, such as football. In small schools, he or she is expected to coach everything.

In small schools the coach may be burdened with many other details and chores. Is there enough equipment and if not, how can the school board purse strings be loosened for more?

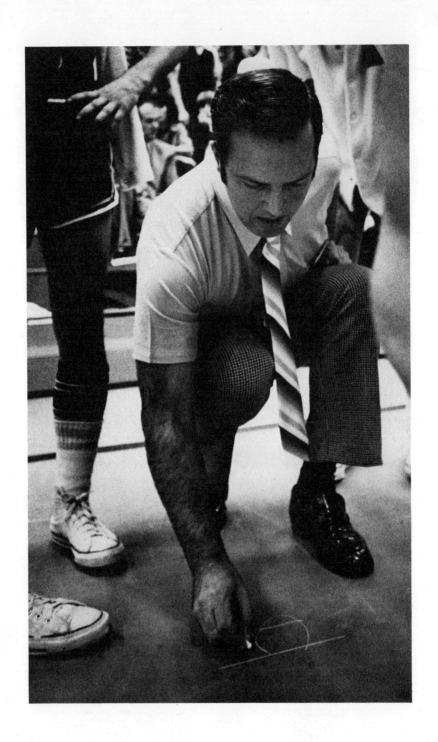

It may even fall to the coach to look after the gym laundry, the electrical service for night games, and arrange for a janitor.

In larger schools, assistants handle these chores. Large colleges and professional teams have managers who see to such details. A stockroom person keeps a record of all the equipment.

Coaches also decide upon plays, or strategy. Those working with small organizations travel to watch other teams perform and once they understand the competition, may change their strategy somewhat. Assistant coaches with larger teams may take over the travel duties.

It's up to the coach to study the performance of the athletes and then make the decision that means joy to some—"You made the varsity team"—and heartbreak to others—"Sorry, but it's the junior varsity for you."

Salaries and benefits

The professional teams pay their coaches huge salaries, perhaps $100,000 a year or more, in addition to certain other benefits. Big colleges pay well, too—$35,000 or more yearly, as well as the benefits the school faculty members receive. But these jobs usually go to the former big-time athletes. That is why the most realistic level for the would-be coach to aim for is level one—a job in a public or private school. Young athletes who didn't make a name for themselves are welcome to work in the school systems. The pay and benefits are at least as high or higher than that of the other teachers in that particular school—probably between $7,500 and $15,000 a year.

A college coach discusses plays and strategy. COURTESY OF ALBANY
DEMOCRAT-HERALD. ALBANY, OREGON

The coach as a teacher

Coaching is quite different from teaching a physical education class where the teacher instructs in the basic techniques
of the sport (see Chapter 12). Actually, the coach takes
over where the physical ed teacher leaves off and gets
down to the finer points of the game and, of course, to
strategy and strengthening teamwork. Coaches at many
schools also teach physical ed classes, and physical ed
teachers coach also.

Personal requirements

What kind of person makes a good coach? It almost goes
without saying that he or she should be in top physical
shape and know thoroughly the sport or sports to be taught.

This high school coach directs a summer football camp. COURTESY
OF ALBANY DEMOCRAT-HERALD. ALBANY, OREGON

Leadership qualities are also called for, otherwise it would be difficult to bring out the best in the athletes and at the same time get them to work together as a team.

And a coach would not remain one for long if the athletes failed to see in him or her qualities of fairness and good judgment. Good moral character rates high, too.

Educational requirements

How can you prepare for a career as a coach? In high school, plan for college and at the same time stay active in the athletic program. Summer jobs in camps working with younger people is fine experience. So is helping your coach as an assistant trainer or manager.

Most high schools insist that their coaches be certified teachers. A bachelor's degree is the minimal requirement. While in college, it is to the future coach's advantage to major in physical education since some states insist upon their coaches having that degree. Playing successfully in the college sport you wish to coach will also be a big plus in your favor.

That first job

After college, or after a time playing professionally, the most likely place to find that first job as a coach is in a high school, grade school, or small college. In larger schools or colleges, the beginner might be able to get a job as an assistant coach. In any case, he or she may teach gym classes and maybe even instruct a classroom subject.

For most well-trained people, there will be a job available after college. This is particularly true for women since athletic programs for girls and women are growing at a fast pace.

50

The climb upward

Getting ahead depends upon how successful your teams are, how well you work with young people, and how you rate with the parents, the public, and fellow coaches.

Some coaches work at the job for many years. Others find the work too physically demanding, once into or past middle age. They may then move into some other area of education or into administration. Others may be into sports-writing or broadcasting, or supervising camps for young people.

6 / Other Sports Officials

All sports depend upon officials to make final decisions about plays and performances. The athletes and fans must recognize the official as honest and knowledgeable. When they don't you'll hear boos and catcalls and an occasional threat like "I'll punch you in the nose!"

Officials work day games and night games; some have to stand on their feet for many hours. They travel a lot, in most cases separately from the athletes. And since their job requires such constant, instant decision-making, they often find the strain exhausting.

But for those who love the games and events, officiating can be a rewarding career.

Though sports would crumble at once without officials to interpret the rules, such jobs are limited, extremely so at the top. Many more opportunities lie at minor league levels, but the pay is minimal.

Another fine area in which to find officiating jobs are schools and colleges where the need for officials in all sports is on an upswing. The sports using the largest number of officials follow.

Students learn how to call a play at this school for umpires. COURTESY AL SOMERS SCHOOL FOR UMPIRES

Baseball

In a major league baseball game there are usually four umpires. One judges from behind home plate, and three make decisions at each of the three bases. Two extra umpires are used in World Series games. There are perhaps forty umpires in each major league under contract, and that's it. Many more work in the minor leagues.

The pay scale rises gradually with the league class. Those starting in the lowest class earn about $700 or $800 a month.

Referees usually have the last word when a coach disputes a call.
COURTESY WESTPORT NEWS, WESTPORT, CONN.

In the major leagues the baseball umpire takes home a fine paycheck (it could go up to $37,000 a year) plus a liberal allowance for travel expense.

If you like baseball officiating enough to look toward it as a professional career, training is recommended. The Al Somers School for Umpires, P.O. Box 2041, Daytona Beach, FL 32015, will send you a free brochure if you write and ask for it.

Football

Several referees—umpires, linesmen, field judges, and back judges—are required for a football game. They are the

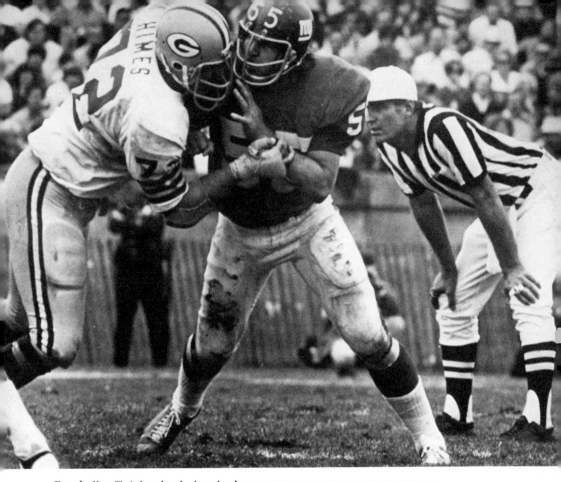

Football officials check for fouls. COURTESY NEW YORK FOOTBALL GIANTS

final authority to settle all disagreements based on rules in the Official's Manual.

Umpires have jurisdiction over equipment, conduct, and actions of players where the team lines up for play—the scrimmage line.

Linesmen operate on one side of the field during the first half of the game and switch to the opposite side during the second half. They check for and report rule violations, and keep track of yardage gained or lost.

Field judges check and judge kicks from the scrimmage

Basketball officials work nearly as hard as the players. COURTESY OF ALBANY DEMOCRAT-HERALD. ALBANY, OREGON

and have other field duties regarding the handling of loose balls.

Back judges operate on the side opposite the linesmen and are responsible for illegal motion, that is, actions that violate the rules.

Big league football officials work under a contract that guarantees them payment—a few hundred dollars for each game—for a certain number of games per season. The big bowl games may bring in $750 to $1000 per game.

Many officials got their training as former players or coaches. Since there are so few playing days, most have other occupations or businesses.

Basketball

A referee and an umpire, assisted by two timers and two scorers are the usual number of officials at a basketball

56

game. Referees inspect and approve all equipment used for keeping score. They conduct the game in accordance with the rules, administer penalties, order time-outs, etc.

Scorers record all the plays, the points scored, and the fouls called on each player.

Timers keep track of all matters regarding time, such as game time and time-outs.

Top basketball officials receive a certain amount of money per game and travel allowances. Officials average two games a week during the season.

Except for the top people in this business, many find it a financial necessity to work at other occupations during the off-season.

Hockey

Eight officials work at a hockey game. A referee and two linesmen are called the major officials. The referee has full control of the game and the final say on everything, including setting the penalties.

The linesmen call violations of rules and report them to the referee. They also have the dangerous job of breaking up fights.

Those called minor officials, whose duties aren't really minor at all, are the two goal judges, the game timekeeper, the penalty timekeeper, and the official scorekeeper. These are unpaid jobs, except during the Stanley Cup playoffs. Residents of the town in which the game is being played take these jobs for the pleasure it gives them.

Trainers

A job as a trainer requires a knowledge of first aid and

Most hockey officials were once players themselves. COURTESY NEW YORK RANGERS

physical therapy. You've probably seen the trainer hop into action the moment there is any indication of an injury. It's the trainer's duty to check and decide whether the player can continue in the game. He or she may have to administer first aid or, if the injury is serious, remove the player from action and see that medical care is provided.

It's an interesting job, and important. But here again, there are only a few such jobs available. They fall into the "middle income" bracket.

The team physician

Many large professional and college teams have a doctor

on the staff. This professional person is there to handle injuries and to decide whether or not an illness is mild enough to permit the athlete to continue playing. If not, it's his or her job to see that the athlete stays out of the game or show and "do what the doctor orders."

The team physician is usually very knowledgeable in "sports medicine," the field that deals specifically with ailments and injuries connected with sports. He or she must have a medical degree, of course, which requires many years of education and training. But for the doctor who has a deep interest in sports, this can be a highly satisfying and well-paying job.

Officiating in other sports

Amateurs who love the sport officiate in most of the other sports not mentioned earlier in this chapter. Timers, judges, etc. in fields such as running and swimming are there because they enjoy being a part of the event, and not for pay. When these and other sports increase in popularity and become "big money" events, there probably will be openings for a few paid officials.

Officiating for amateur events doesn't necessarily lead to a professional career, but all experience helps.

7 / Golf and Tennis Everyone?

Golf and tennis are the IN sports. It seems almost everyone plays one or the other now, has in the past, or will in the future.

Golf

The tournament golfer

Nearly 300 professional golfers travel from course to course competing for prize money that adds up to more than seven million dollars each year. These traveling golfers follow the sun by playing tournaments in warm locations during January. Early spring finds them playing further north, and it's New England and the Midwest by summer. When the leaves fall, they are back in California and Nevada.

There are over forty major tournaments a year, and smaller ones that are held nearby at the same time for those golfers who don't quite qualify for the bigger one. The players pay their own expenses—travel, hotel, caddie fees, entry fees, etc.—that might add up to $300 to $400 a week. At least twice as many golfers may try to get in (qualify) as there are openings in a tournament. Those who do make it may be dropped or "cut" after playing 36 holes. If so, they pay their bills and hope for better luck next time.

Those who do make it share huge sums of prize money known as "the purse." The winner usually gets about 20 percent. If the purse is $100,000, he or she is handed a check for about $20,000. Eleven percent, or $11,000 goes to the second place winner. The share of the purse is very small for those out of the top spots. Most do not earn enough to pay their expenses.

Sometimes an individual or group will sponsor a golfer they believe shows promise. They will pay the expenses hoping that he or she will be successful someday and they will then share in the rewards.

Those who wind up often in the winner's circle may earn over $200,000 a year. These top players become celebrities and add to their fortune in the ways other star athletes do. (See Chapter 2). With so much money at stake, golfers have become highly-disciplined businesspeople.

The golf pro

Most of the people who make a career in golf do so as instructors. There are about 12,000 golf courses in the United States, and over eleven million players. Even some of those with creaky bones and poor health manage to play golf into old age. Almost all of these people take lessons at some time or another either to learn the game or improve it. Most often, these lessons are taught by the "golf pro"— there are 12,000 or so who hold this position. About the same number work as assistants or instructors, full or part

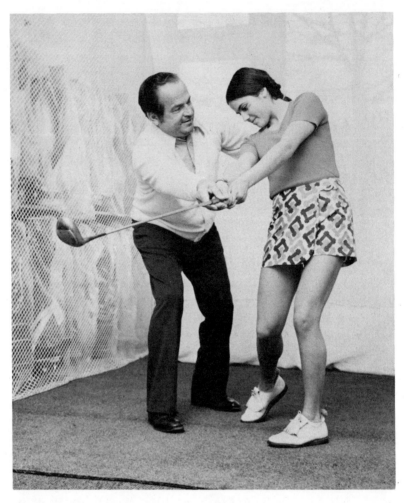

This golf pro instructs at his golf school during the winter months.
COURTESY NICK ROBERTO. GREENWICH, CONN.

time. These people work at a private or city golf club, or at a driving range.

Pros are approved by the Professional Golfers Association after taking a course at the PGA school in Florida.

Classes there include the study of grass (the types and disease control) and business courses such as accounting. Only the top 15 students are awarded the PGA card permitting them to be a golf pro. Those who finish out of the top fifteen spots may try again at a later time.

Duties at the club usually involve handling the entire golfing program. But the pro starts by serving a five-year apprenticeship as an assistant at a club.

The head pro's salary is very small, but he earns extra money by giving lessons and selling golf clubs and other equipment at the pro shop. He may earn a lot of money or a small amount, depending upon his business skill and his willingness to work.

In the North, the golf pro may have to turn to other jobs during the cold winter months. Many times good golfers find assistant pro jobs where they are able to practice the game and improve their skills. Then they may try for a playing career. Only a few will make it. But those who don't at least have a job to return to.

One-time successful golfers, especially those who are well-known, often are hired by a resort hotel to teach guests or to play a few rounds with them. It is a public relations position and serves to publicize the resort and to attract more customers.

Many young people caddy and learn more of the fine points of the game (as well as extra money). Caddies also are entitled to use the course free or at cut-rates during slow periods.

Tennis

Tennis began as a gentle form of recreation and has been

The fantastic growth in the popularity of tennis has opened the doors for many more instructors, or tennis pros. COURTESY GREENWICH RACQUET CLUB. GREENWICH, CONN.

around for over a hundred years. Only recently has it become a big sport with its share of celebrity players and television coverage. And it's a sport that continues to grow in popularity. Thousands are added to the active list each year until now there are at least 14 million tennis players in this country over the age of fifteen. A half billion dollars a year is spent on this game, for everything from balls to ball-serving machines.

Professionals who play the tournament circuits find purses nearly as large as in golf. They are divided among the winners in much the same way. And these players have

64

an advantage over golfers since many of the 110,000 courts are now inside, may stay open all night, and weather need not necessarily affect the playing schedule.

The fantastic growth in the popularity of tennis has resulted in courts sprouting up like hamburger stands all over the country. This has opened the doors for many more tennis instructors, or tennis pros. They work in a similar way to the golf pro—teaching and earning commissions by handling merchandise in the pro shop. They often live a gypsy kind of life—traveling from southern tennis clubs in the winter to northern ones in the summer. But again, with inside courts, they may now sink their roots in one place and call it home.

Many well-known tennis players become the instructor, or pro, at a club at a good salary when his or her playing days are over.

Other good tennis players find employment at tennis camps where over 100,000 adults spend at least one week of their vacation time each year. There are more than 100 tennis camps for children, too, where the going rate for admission is $500 per week.

Another career is managing a court or camp. Those who do this know and like the game, but they are good business people, too.

Officials

Officials at the game include the umpire who is paid a small fee for working a meet. A few, on fairly good salaries, dash by plane with the athletes from one match to another on the pro tour.

Each game also requires nine or ten judges but these jobs are performed for little or no pay.

Netting the breaks

Some tennis clubs and camps hire college students to help teach during vacations from school. Younger people may do other chores in exchange for lessons and court time. Both of these places offer opportunities for you who hope to make tennis playing, officiating, or instructing a career.

8 / The World of Horses

Love horses? Many people thrill to the sight, smell, and touch of them. If you are one of those, then perhaps you have thought how exciting it would be to work with these marvelous animals. Fortunately, in the field of sports involving horses, the door is open to many careers.

Thoroughbred horse racing

Horse racing has been called "the sport of kings." Today it is supported by so many of us commoners that it has grown to be the biggest spectator sport. Nearly 70 million viewers a year not only enjoy watching racing at the track but get great delight out of placing bets on the outcome.

The career that seems most obvious is that of rider. The jockey is pictured astride the horse in the winner's circle, surrounded by a cheering throng. We thrill to the news that the race has earned the jockey several thousand dollars. What a way to spend an afternoon, we think, with perhaps a trace of envy. But the competition is so great, only a handful—fewer than a hundred—of the 1500 jockeys rid-

Thoroughbred horse racing is this country's biggest spectator sport. The jockey riding the winning horse in this race is a woman.
COURTESY NEW YORK RACING ASSOCIATION. BOB COGLIANESE

ing the 20,000 or more racehorses in this country enjoy such financial rewards.

This career is limited to excellent riders who are small, wiry, daring, and weigh no more than 108 pounds. But if you are the right size and would like to be a jockey, begin as soon as possible to work at a stable near your home, or at a racetrack if there is one nearby.

To start training, a would-be jockey must be at least sixteen years of age. He or she is placed, with parental consent, in the care of a licensed thoroughbred horse owner who supervises the training. This will probably mean living away from home.

Students are taught how to sit on a racehorse, to judge timing and pacing, and how to handle the high strung, powerful thoroughbred horses. Like the professionals, they live a quiet and sober life for they must keep very fit.

But before and during this time of learning, jockeys work from sunrise to sunset as stablehands, doing such chores as cleaning out the stalls and rubbing down the horses on a track until the trainer feels he or she is ready to enter a race.

Training may take from one to three years, and it is only after riding forty winners that the trainee is considered an apprentice jockey and permitted to ride in races with more experienced jockeys.

The student is licensed, as is the jockey, by a racing authority and must abide by all the rules of racing.

Only a few become successful enough to be able to avoid menial stable chores. But even the top ones work hard to keep fit. The day begins with the jockeys galloping horses from sunrise to midmorning. They may continue with other exercises throughout the day when they are not racing. But the rewards for such work can pay off in a big way. The best known jockeys—the celebrities—have amassed fortunes through riding.

A horse, its jockey, trainer, stablehands, and perhaps owner, work at the same track and live nearby for about six or ten weeks. This keeps all of them from having to move to the point of exhaustion. They race summers in the North and winters in the South.

The jockeys, when they are not riding during a race, are kept in a room where they are not permitted to speak to trainers or owners. (This practice was started to prevent

69

anyone from trying to "fix" the outcome of a race.) Jockeys can relax, take steam baths, and watch the other races on television.

A central organization plays a major role in thoroughbred racing—registering 25,000 foals by name each year, for example. A large number of office workers and executives oversee the many details. You may write to this organization for free detailed information for apprentice jockeys: The Jockey Club, 300 Park Avenue, New York, New York 10022.

Trainers

Many former jockeys become trainers. So do veterinarians, stablehands, farmers, or people who simply love horses. Trainers are not prepared for the job in a formal way.

The best trainers work under contracts for horse owners who are in racing for the sport. They earn a salary that may range up to $30 or $40 thousand a year. In addition, they get a percentage of the winnings of their horses, usually ten percent. This may add up to a small fortune.

Public trainers are those who train horses for different owners and are not under contract to any one person or group. They may handle as many as thirty horses for several owners. They receive a certain amount of money each day and out of that they pay for food and equipment. Public trainers, too, may receive a percentage of the winnings.

Harness horse racing

In this form of horse racing, each competing horse pulls a light-weight, two-wheeled vehicle called a sulky, which is manned by a skilled driver. There are two kinds of com-

In harness racing, the horse pulls a two-wheeled sulky which is manned by a skilled driver. One driver earned over $2 million in one year. COURTESY YONKERS RACEWAY

petition—races for trotting horses and races for pacing horses. These horses are of a breed that is stronger and easier to handle than the high-strung thoroughbred.

Unlike the jockeys just mentioned, this driver isn't up there on the horse's back so size is not so important. What's needed is courage, nerve, and a feeling for the reins. (In 1937 a girl of eleven took a trotter on the track and smashed a track record.)

Many horse-loving people are buying harness racehorses

for this increasingly popular sport because they can, if they have the talent for it, experience the thrill of getting into the sulky and driving it themselves. They needn't turn the job over to someone else. Many do, of course.

Training and practice bring the best drivers to the surface and they get the most and best opportunities to drive.

This racing season gets underway in April or May. Trainers, owners, and drivers, with their animals and equipment, follow the circuit for at least 20 weeks and cover 15,000 miles.

Purses of about $24 million are awarded each year to the owners of winning horses. The driver shares in the winnings.

Those who ride in the Grand Circuit, which is the "major league" of harness racing, have a chance to earn millions. Those who ride at the 800 minor tracks earn considerably less.

The rodeo

"Ya-hoo-ooo!" the rider shouts as he races into the arena. Smells of animals, straw, and hay fill the air, but it isn't the wild West. It could be New York or Atlanta or any other large city in the United States or Canada where some 600 rodeos are held each year. Today more than ten million persons attend these events annually.

The rodeo had its beginning in the sweat, toil, and dust of the American western range. Its events, such as calf roping and saddle bronc riding, developed not from play, as did most sports, but from the cowboy's everyday work.

More than 3,000 cowboys, all members of the Rodeo Cowboys Association, travel the rodeo circuit at their own expense. Members of the Girls Rodeo Association compete

72

Rodeo events developed not from play, as did most sports, but from the cowboys' everyday work. COURTESY RODEO COWBOYS ASSOCIATION

in certain events also. Entry fees of up to $100 are charged —money that is often added to the rodeo purse. Competition events for younger people are growing increasingly popular. Riders also perform at state and county fairs.

Prize money adds up to over five million dollars a year. The winners in different events win several thousand dollars each. The losers gain nothing but experience. Some contenders enter over 100 rodeos a year and the very best ones earn over $50,000 annually at this dangerous sport.

Successful rodeo performers, it seems, have to begin training at an early age for most events. Growing up and working on a ranch provides the best background. Today's rodeo cowboys keep in excellent physical shape and are often college-educated.

There are rodeo schools, too, where training uses such modern-day devices as a mechanical bucking machine. Television cameras using videotape instant replay equipment let the cowboy see the flaws in his or her own performance.

Horse shows

Horse shows have an enormous impact on the entire horse population. Without these competitive events, and their prizes and awards, it is likely that breeders, exhibitors, and riders would have lost interest long ago in their horse-related activities. Horses, aside from those used for ranch work and racing, would probably have disappeared. Certain breeds would be a thing of the past and others would not have developed to their present extent.

Various types of shows offer a chance for competition among riders of all types and at every stage of learning. Most camps, riding clubs and schools, and private schools with riding programs, hold shows of one type or another from time to time for their members. Riding contests of an unusual and fun type, called gymkhanas, are introduced early in the teaching program. There is also competition in

Horse and rider have trained many years for this jump. COURTESY OF ABC SPORTS

stable management, knowledge of first aid for horses, and other areas of horse care. Later, young riders enter the accepted horsemanship competition.

Owning show horses has been called a rich person's sport since the prizes won seldom make up for the money needed to train and support a horse and transport it to the various shows. There are, however, huge sums of money paid to a breeder for a great stallion or mare he or she may have developed.

All shows except those approved by the American Horse Show Association are called unrecognized shows. The A.H.S.A. makes the rules, selects and approves judges, and

75

organizes shows on a national basis. Entry fees are added to the purse and divided among the winners in the various divisions and classes.

Competitions patterned after the Olympic trials in Europe are growing more popular each year. These meets are the only source this country has to draw upon for its Olympic equestrian teams.

Giving a show requires a lot of work. Committees must be organized to handle such things as the program, publicity, and prizes.

Some judges and stewards are paid for judging a horse show. Others receive only transportation and expense money and a thank-you gift.

Other positions

Whatever your experience or training with horses, it need not go to waste if for some reason (such as a jockey growing too big) you have to drop the occupation you want or have. There are many other positions that could use your particular skills.

Teaching is the largest area of employment. And in addition to the positions discussed already, there are racetrack, show, and rodeo managers; stable managers, hands, and grooms; horse transportation operators; dealers of horses; saddlers; vendors of horse feed, equipment and riding apparel; photographers and writers specializing in horses (see Chapter 11); and auctioneers of horses and equipment.

Shows, rodeos, and racetracks may employ veterinarians, announcers, ringmasters, gate attendants, ring clerks, starters, timekeepers, blacksmiths, and show secretaries, besides, of course, people to handle office chores. For some, this is likely to be part-time work.

All shows use people to promote the performance and handle public relations. (See Chapter 4).

Horse show and rodeo managers may profit or lose from the venture, as any other person might who is in the business of running a show.

9 / Boxing

Prizefighting in America began as an exhibition in theaters about a hundred years ago. Since then it has become a worldwide, favorite sport. It has not lost its theatrical appeal. Television has made it a favorite form of entertainment.

Over the years, eight divisions have been developed for fighters: heavyweight, light-heavyweight, middleweight, welterweight, lightweight, featherweight, bantamweight, and flyweight. According to the rules of the National Boxing Association (N.B.A.) only fighters falling into the same weight division may fight each other. World championship titles go to the best in each category.

The boxer

Heavyweight championship boxing offers purses to the winner that King Midas would envy. And cameras are there during the payoff for all to witness. Boxing matches in the lighter weight divisions are often fought for huge purses, too.

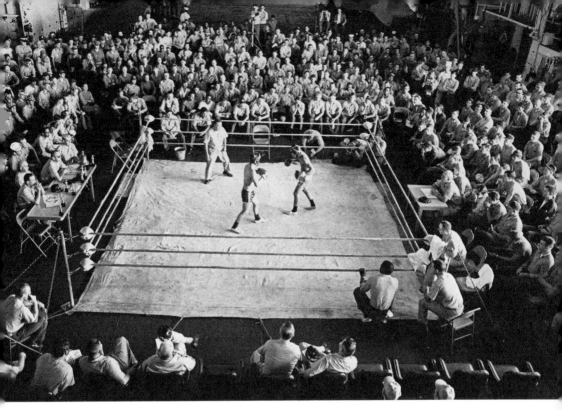

Boxing is a popular sport around the world. This match is taking place aboard an aircraft carrier near China. COURTESY U.S. NAVY

But boxing is a sport that will reward only the very, very best with a well-paying career. For the others, it is often the road to nowhere with nothing to show for the tough work, the travel from one small town to another, and the pain of training, but a battered and scarred body. The brain, too, may suffer permanent injury.

Even those who had some success often wind up broke and soon disappear from the memory of the public. For such people, finding a new way of earning a living is very difficult, especially if they neglected their education in favor of boxing.

Still there are those who are willing to give this sport a try, hoping for the success that can bring so much fame and fortune. But only those who succeed at amateur boxing should attempt to climb the long road to the top.

The money paid beginning boxers is very small. The little clubs may pay no more than $50 for four rounds. And a fight a week may be all you'll get. The boxer good enough to be featured as the main event may get $1000 or more.

At the bigger fight clubs, like Madison Square Garden and others where the main bout is televised, the boxers may get several thousand dollars. As you know, a few who have become stars fight one bout for a million or more—dollars, that is!

The amateur

Amateur boxing, with its careful supervision, is the only way to start. Many organizations such as police departments and boys' clubs volunteer their time to train young people.

The Golden Gloves tournaments are the best-known amateur boxing events. Here, local tournaments are followed by championship matches. The object of the Golden Gloves, in which thousands of boys compete each year, is to build the boys' bodies and characters. But many world champions, including Joe Louis and Rocky Marciano, have come up through Golden Gloves.

The Amateur Athletic Union of the United States (A.A.U.) holds contests, too, and the Pan American and the Olympic tryouts are held every four years. There are also worldwide Army, Navy, and Air Force championships.

As yet, very few women participate in this sport.

If a boy emerges a winner in amateur matches, he will be encouraged to turn pro. If that should happen to you, think it over carefully. If you decide that this is the turn you wish your life to take, talk about it with professional boxers

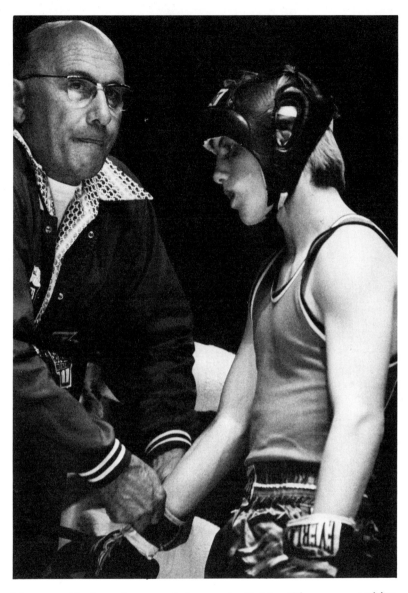

Many world champions get their start in Golden Gloves competition.
COURTESY ALBANY DEMOCRAT-HERALD. ALBANY, OREGON

and others in the business whom you respect. There are
many disreputable people in boxing—make certain that
you don't place your future in the hands of one of them.

The referee watches to make certain the boxers observe the rules.
COURTESY ABC SPORTS

Finding a good and decent manager should be your primary concern. If a prospective manager offers you a guarantee amounting to a thousand dollars or more, this will show his good faith in your future.

The manager

The manager's hope is that someday the boxer will win some big purses and he will have a share of them. But until then, his job is a gamble. He teaches the techniques of the sport, trains and supports, provides the boxer with the necessities of boxing such as equipment and fees and traveling expenses. He will do his best to get matches for which

82

the boxer is suited. He'll aim for bouts that offer big purses.

The manager's hope is that someday you will win some big purses. Usually one-third of the winnings is his share. A good manager is worth it.

Many managers once were professional or amateur boxers or had experience in some other activity related to boxing, but this does not necessarily have to be a part of the manager's background. A few have come from such unrelated fields as business and law.

A job as manager can be an interesting one for those who find boxing a fascinating sport but who don't wish to or can't participate in it themselves.

Referee

The referee is the only person aside from the boxers allowed in the ring during the rounds. He gives final instructions about the rules and enforces them. If he believes a boxer is outclassed, or injured, he may stop the bout and declare the other contestant the winner. In case of a knockdown, or knockout, he counts over the fallen fighter. He keeps score, by a system agreed upon before the fight —usually certain points for specific punches and for their effectiveness.

Judges

Two judges sit on opposite sides of the ring during the fight. They keep score, round by round, in the same way as the referee.

Ring announcer

The ring announcer introduces the contestants, gives their

weights and other information about the fighters and officials. At the end of the bout, the winner is announced.

Timekeeper

This person keeps track of the rounds, which are three minutes each, and the rest periods, which are one minute long.

Seconds

Before a bout, a second bandages the hands of the boxer and takes care of the wants of the fighter during the rest periods between bouts. A knowledge of first aid is necessary.

Physician

It is a rule of the National Boxing Association (N.B.A.) that every contestant must be examined by an especially licensed physician. This person stays at ringside during the bouts to remain aware of the physical fitness of contestants at all times. The boxers are examined before every fight. After the bout, they are examined and given whatever medical treatment is necessary.

Those working at the jobs mentioned except for the manager are usually paid by the fight. The physician and the referee earn the most, which may range from a few dollars at a small club to several hundred at a larger one. The others make considerably less.

10 / Broadcasting Sports

The thought has probably crossed your mind that broadcasting sports news or doing play-by-play on radio or television would be a great way to earn a living, and it is. Most of those who do find the job exciting and creative. There is also the opportunity to become a national personality and earn a great deal of money. As with all such desirable jobs, there are bound to be far more applicants than there are openings available. But don't let that stop you from trying. Just keep on practicing and learning.

The employers

Some sportscasters work for radio or television stations or national networks. Some are employed by athletic teams. Network announcers must not show favoritism, and local stations will discourage you from favoring the home team too obviously. If you are employed by the team, you will be expected to slant your comments slightly in favor of your organization. But no one likes to hear a sportscaster who is too slanted, even if it's in favor of the team one is cheering for.

Regardless of the employer, it is the announcer's job to make each game or event sound as exciting as possible.

The sports staff

For radio sports coverage, the staff is usually made up of two announcers, a producer, and an engineer. One announcer may call the game, doing play-by-play, and the other provides color—that is, offers interesting comments about the team, players, and the game or event. (For major sports and broadcasts this person may be a former athlete rather than an announcer.) The two announcers often switch duties midway during the broadcast.

The producer handles all details related to production, such as seeing the commercials go on as scheduled. An engineer supervises the sound and technical matters of the broadcast.

Television sports broadcasting uses other technical people such as camera operators and videotape engineers. But again, two announcers make up the team most often used. The staff for the big network broadcasts also may include a full-time statistician. (More about those duties in Chapter 4).

For major sports, a press information kit is often given to the staff each day (by the PR department mentioned in Chapter 4). This contains all the latest news and statistics. During the game, announcers also give the scores of other games.

Announcers working for small stations are more or less on their own. The job of calling the game or event smoothly and colorfully can be much more difficult, but then, without so much sponsor's money riding on your performance, the pressure isn't as great. An announcer at a smaller

Sportscasters are located in the broadcasting booth high above the crowd at the stadium. COURTESY NATIONAL BROADCASTING COMPANY, INC.

station might welcome the offer of help with color and statistics from a student who knows the game and players.

Some sportscasters use spotters to help identify players, especially during football games. But most of the top announcers prefer to cut out the middleman and do the job themselves, thereby lowering the risk of mistakes. Consequently, they work long hours, as professional spotters do, memorizing names, numbers, and positions. They become familiar with the appearance, walk, and gestures of

87

the different players so they can recognize each at once, even when mud-soaked uniforms make the athletes look identical.

Play-by-play

Play-by-play announcers must be glib talkers. The radio listener sees the event through words so your description must be accurate and at the same time evoke a vivid mental picture. Not quite so much glib talk is necessary on television. In fact, too much can be annoying. But still, the viewer expects the announcer to help him or her understand the action and identify the players.

Many sportscasters who do play-by-play, even those who are successful, practice with a tape recorder. They turn off the television sound and report the action, be it in the arena, field, or rink. They search for new ways to describe a person running, throwing, or whatever. They play back their own tape recording and then seek ways to improve their performance. Try the same thing yourself. Your first attempts will be clumsy, but don't get discouraged. Every announcer is disappointed with his or her first efforts. But with practice you will notice improvement. And it does take practice—hours and hours, year after year.

The working day

Sportscasters arrive well ahead of the scheduled event time to check lineups, pronunciation of athlete's names, and any other important data with managers or team captains. They review the contents of the press information kit so that the rules, records, and other "color information" is fresh in their minds.

88

This sportscaster reports the news in sports for television audiences.
COURTESY N.B.C. SPORTS

When they seat themselves in the broadcasting booth, they arrange their scoring and spotting charts so that everything is easy to see and handle. Any written information received from the team or athletes is gone over, too, and checked for inclusion in the broadcast.

The actual broadcast is difficult and demanding, but if you're at the top in this profession, you will have a large staff to help you. Still, you're the captain of this team, and the success of the broadcast rests mostly on your shoulders.

Sports reporting

Writing sports news for radio and television is similar to that of newspaper reporting, but you have to learn how to write interesting, informative copy for the ear, rather than the eye. Sometimes it's necessary for you to go out and "dig" a bit for unusual stories and little-known facts that will make your report a cut above the others. A recorded interview (called a "voicer" or "actuality") inserted into your broadcast adds a great deal of interest. Interviews, even with some of the top athletes, are usually not difficult to get. After all, they benefit from the publicity, too.

Sports reports run about five minutes of air time. Much of the material used will be wire copy, that is, written material that reaches the station over a teletype machine. These wire services give more sport news than you would ever use. It's your job to select what you want and edit it. You'll have to get the facts yourself and write your own reports regarding local sport news.

The wire service also supplies short feature stories about all kinds of sports that you may use in your radio broadcast. During the season a sport is active—for example, baseball—reports will center on that sport. Features would deal with something like World Series history.

Certain wire services transmit still photographs of sports events, too. These and films and video tapes supplied by the networks may also be worked into your broadcast.

Preparation

To be a sportscaster you should first train to be a good announcer. Another book we have written, "Prepare for a Career in Radio and Television Announcing," will advise you about that in a detailed way. But here are some general suggestions. Get as much education as you possibly can. Add to your vocabulary constantly, since words are a basic tool of the announcer. In high school, pay special attention to your English, Speech, writing and journalism classes. Extra-curricular activities such as drama and debate are helpful. If you are fortunate enough to attend a high school that has its own radio station or club and perhaps even a television studio, take advantage of that. Spend every moment you can before the microphone and camera.

Select a college that offers a degree in communication, or one where you will at least be able to participate in radio and television programs.

Work closely with your athletic directors and the athletes. Try to get stories and interviews. Then do your reports, just as professionals do.

On the air

Sportscasters and reporters most often start out at a small radio station. They handle all local sporting events from the high school basketball game to summer boat races. Before applying for a job, learn all you can about every sport, even those that might bore you.

The smaller the station, the less money you will earn. Sports announcers start at minimal salaries—less than $200 a week.

There are over 7,000 radio stations in the United States. If in need of a sports announcer, a radio station often advertises in the "help wanted" section of a magazine called *Broadcasting*. When you believe you are ready to apply for a job, check the listings in the magazine. Your town library probably has a copy. It may take some time before a radio station will consider hiring you, and then the position offered may be far from where you would like to live. But in announcing, you have to start wherever you can land that first job.

Sometimes a local radio station hires young, interested

people to assist their regular sports staff. This would also be an excellent way to get your foot on the first rung of this career ladder.

There are fewer than 900 television stations and most of those are only willing to hire someone who has had professional experience at another television station or in radio. The pay in television is higher and in many ways the job is more demanding. The practical way to head for a television career is to get your start in radio and move on from there. Many sportscasters, of course, alternate doing both radio and television work.

Your big competition

The really top sportscasting jobs in television today often go to the former big-time athletes. This is because broadcast officials and sponsors of programs believe that the "name" athlete will draw viewers. This practice will change only if the sponsor decides more people would watch the game and enjoy it with a trained, articulate announcer calling the shots.

Those athletes who make the effort to learn the art of announcing usually succeed. If they depend only upon their name for success, they are almost certain to fail.

11 / Reporting, Writing, and Photography

Have you ever been to a game and looked into the press box? Perhaps there was a swirl of activity, but then again, all you may have seen were some relaxed observers with note pads and pencils. But still you noticed that the people working there usually can come and go into the dugout or locker room as they wish, can chat easily with the players and are, in other words, very involved in the sports scene.

Jobs in short supply

Perhaps you envied them for their easy access to the excitement and thrills of the events they're paid to watch and write about, and would like such a job for yourself. If so, it is certainly one worth aiming for. But only those who care enough about it to work hard and stick to it will ever make it. Why? First of all, there are far fewer newspapers than people who would like to write for them. If you live in a small town, there is probably only one. That paper may hire a sports reporter but it is likely that he or she will be assigned to cover other kinds of stories, too. One

A sportswriter interviews a celebrity in a golf match. COURTESY
SPORTS ILLUSTRATED

job—and there may be dozens besides yourself who would
like to claim it.

The sportswriter's life

Sportswriting for a small paper can be a fairly relaxed way

94

to earn a living. The pay isn't going to make anyone rich, but there's a certain prestige to this job that offers both variety and excitement.

Life can be hectic and demanding for sports reporters who write for the large city papers, magazines, and the syndicated columns. The syndicated columns are concerned with sports on a national level and the same story is printed in papers in different parts of the country. But unlike the small newspapers, the large ones can offer a full time and well-paying position.

Reporters often travel with the teams. While adjusting to swift changes in time and climate, food, scenery, and living quarters, they still must write a story and get it in on time.

This routine continues all during the playing season. Then the writer may be assigned to cover another sport, and the whirlwind routine continues.

The chances are the readers saw the game on television or heard it on radio. They know the score and the statistics, so the writer must strive to enlighten the readers with the background, observations, and new information. At the same time, the reports must be colorful and dramatic, perhaps humorous, too. And it should not be so simple that it will insult knowledgeable sports fans, but not so filled with technical terms that only the experts will understand it.

The background you'll need

It's almost impossible today to get a sportswriting job without a college education. But college isn't important just for journalism courses. The other subjects you will study there—psychology, history, business, art—will prove invaluable since sports relate in some ways to all areas of life and living.

Here are some things you can do now. Start working on your school paper, and not just at sportswriting. The skills of reporting, copy reading, editing, and headline writing that you will learn are the same ones you'll use later when working professionally.

Increase your vocabulary. Words are your tools and you must use them skillfully to put a story together, just as a carpenter must handle his hammer skillfully to put up a building.

Study the sports pages of newspapers. Try to figure out why some stories appeal to you more than others. Discuss this with your English teacher. Among other things, it will probably be pointed out that the writers whose work you enjoy most have a rich vocabulary, select words that excite, such as active verbs, and string the words together into interesting sentences.

Another plus would be the ability to take pictures of professional quality to illustrate your stories, so perhaps you could look into photography now as an extra-curricular activity.

That first job

After college, how do you get started? Some people break in by answering "help wanted" ads in *Editor and Publisher*. This is a trade magazine for writers which also has a "situations wanted" section where you may put in your application for a job. The magazine is found at most large newsstands and in public libraries.

You might also try for a position at your local paper. Perhaps the editor would be willing to let you come in as an assistant to the sportswriter, though it's more likely you'd start as a copy person. But that's a beginning. Don't pass it by.

A few young men and women get work at a newspaper doing simple tasks while still in college, and upon graduation step into a full-time job.

Sometimes college students become stringers for larger newspapers. This means writing stories of campus activities which include sporting events. Most stringers are selected from those working on the college paper.

Established sportswriters usually discover better jobs listed in *Editor and Publisher* and move up the career ladder that way. Sometimes editors will seek out writers they admire and invite them to join their staffs.

Sportswriters, like television sports reporters, sometimes become celebrities. But unlike the star athlete, the writer-reporter may stay at this job for a lifetime, and that's an advantage many an athlete envies.

Photographers

A sports photographer understands all the things that go to make a good picture, such as lighting, composition, and color. But unlike many other photographers, this person has to be agile and very alert, for the job requires that he or she be in the thick of the action. Sports photographers must capture the action and drama of players and officials as well as the emotions of the fans on the still or movie film. Posed pictures are seldom of interest to sports fans.

The photographer should also have the ability to write interesting copy, for at the very least, he or she is often called upon to write captions for the pictures explaining what they are about or identifying the people and plays.

97

Sports photographers must capture the action and drama. Posed pictures are seldom of interest to fans. COURTESY ALBANY DEMOCRAT-HERALD. ALBANY, OREGON

College isn't essential for this career, but it would be a good idea if you aim for a college education similar to that of reporter and writer.

If photography is a hobby of yours, join a school or local camera club now. Your school coaches and physical education instructors would no doubt encourage you to take pictures of the activities they supervise. Once you feel your pictures are of professional quality, show them to the sports editor of your hometown paper. Many college students sell pictures to that source, and sometimes capable high school students break into the field of sports photography that way, too.

12 / Physical Education Teachers

You enjoy sports and athletics or you wouldn't have this book in your hands. Do you also enjoy working with people? Would you like your working day to be active and varied? If so, it would be very worth your while to look into teaching physical education either in school systems or in the field of recreation.

The school systems

The need for certain teachers in private and public school systems seems to be on the decrease for now, but the demand for physical education teachers still runs high. And the outlook remains good.

Grade school instructors teach simple exercises as well as more organized sports activities. In high schools and colleges, they are involved in a wide variety of events and oversee competition at all levels within schools and between schools.

In addition to teaching athletics and sports, the "Phys

100

A high school physical education teacher referees a wrestling match.
COURTESY OF ALBANY DEMOCRAT-HERALD. ALBANY, OREGON

Ed" teacher may also coach. Other duties may include assisting in the scheduling of sports events, figuring out the money needed for sports equipment, giving first aid to

101

A student at a junior college follows the directions of her gymnastics teacher. COURTESY ALBANY DEMOCRAT-HERALD. ALBANY, OREGON

injured students, and determining an athlete's place in a sports activity. Many teach classroom courses. Often these are in the field of health education or hygiene.

College teachers may specialize in teaching one sport.

Rewards

Working conditions in this career field are usually good. Some night and weekend work and some travel may be called for, especially for those who coach. (Check the chapter on coaches for specific duties in that field.)

Physical education teachers receive the same benefits and earn about the same as the others working in that particular school system—about $7,500 to $12,000 a year in elementary and high schools. College physical education teachers earn more. Extra money is paid for coaching. The amount is based on the time spent, the responsibility, public pressure involved, and the experience and education of the instructor.

The athletic director

An athletic director may be in charge of a school or a school district's athletic program. He or she works under guidelines set by the principal or the superintendent of schools. This is a top, executive position paying $12,000 a year up to $40,000 or more, depending on the duties, the location, and the size and importance of the school athletic program. Those who reach this level have had experience on the playing field, or as a coach, or as a physical education instructor, or all three.

Athletic directors have huge responsibilities. They make contacts with other schools and athletic organizations. But they also deal with non-school agencies such as police and fire departments, medical and safety associations. For example, they must make certain they have enough police officers to help with crowd control and traffic at games. They may oversee scheduling, arrange transportation and insurance for the players, work on the budget, and supervise and evaluate the performance of coaches and others who work in the physical education department.

A college student disagrees with the decision of his physical educa-tion teacher. COURTESY OF ALBANY DEMOCRAT-HERALD. ALBANY, OREGON

Athletic directors work closely with architects and planning committees regarding the building of new sports facilities or the remodeling of old ones. They provide the practical knowledge needed for the proper layout of such facilities as locker rooms and athletic fields.

Developing a group of dependable assistants to assume specific responsibilities is absolutely essential.

Obviously, the high demands made upon athletic directors in so many areas require that he or she be able to build close working relationships with other people. A working knowledge of business and finance would help here, too.

Many physical education teachers work in the field of recreation. This woman teaches paddle tennis, as well as other athletic activities, for the YWCA. COURTESY POLLY MEMHARD. RIVERSIDE, CONN.

The recreational field

Government leaders are beginning to realize the importance of directing our free time in healthful and worthwhile ways. So community recreation centers, many large businesses, and government and military organizations include sports as part of their planned leisure-time activity.

Trained recreation leaders who head these programs—for community centers, youth organizations, and the Armed Forces, to name but a few—often find need for

105

physical education graduates to handle sports. They may also hire other personnel to oversee other activities such as arts and crafts or music. Sometimes they hire specialists who may teach or direct only one sport—swimming, for example.

Physical education teachers in the recreational field usually work a regular 40-hour week. Beginning salaries range from $9,000 to $20,000. Part-time work is available especially during the summer and pays from the minimum scale up to $6.00 an hour.

Since most people in the recreational field are young and the programs are constantly expanding, the move upward to supervisor or director or their assistants can be swift.

Your personal qualifications

The physical education teacher needs to be in good health and, like all good teachers, have a genuine interest in other people and the ability to get along with them. Athletic skills are necessary of course, and an interest in all sports. So are traits such as reliability, patience, and good judgment.

Education and training

You'll need at least a bachelor's degree from college to succeed in this kind of work. Education beyond that is necessary for college level teaching and for many of the executive positions such as athletic director. Each state has its own requirements, so check with your guidance counselor to make certain you start running on the right track.

106

Over 400 colleges and universities have four or five year curriculums in physical education. A list of these schools will be sent to you for the asking. Write: American Association of Health, Physical Education and Recreation, 1202 16th Street, N.W., Washington, D.C., 20036.

If you're not now involved in your school's sports program, join up at once. Another helpful extracurricular activity is public speaking.

13 / A Little Bit
About a Lot of Things

If we failed to mention many favorite sports, it is because in certain areas there is no structured establishment or business that can promise regular or lasting employment. There are still teaching and coaching jobs available, of course, and nearly all sports support businesses that sell or rent equipment. There are also training clubs or camps that these sports enthusiasts might operate. But for the most part, opportunities for earning a good living over a period of time, with opportunities to someday use the acquired skills in related activities, are too slim to be highly recommended. (Sky-diving and swimming might be good examples.)

Of course almost every competitive sports event offers some financial rewards for the winners in the form of prize money, or the purse. A skinny one may contain only a few dollars; a fat one a hundred thousand or more.

When the television cameras roll out to cover an event, the purse is likely to bulge. That's the way it's been with skiing, for example. There's a lot of money riding on the backs of the downhill racers and ski jumpers you see on TV.

Skiers compete for huge purses, especially when the event is broad-cast on television as this one is. COURTESY ABC SPORTS

Now let's have a look at some other sports careers that seem to have a number of negative sides to them.

Automobile racing

In no other sports career does the hand of death reach out so often as it does to the driver in championship car racing. But these events do provide a testing ground for the latest in automotive design and road safety. The car manufacturers apply the knowledge gained to the cars we eventually purchase.

Only those of you who have a deep love for automobiles should consider driving as a career. And even then, there's

Members of an auto racing team make a last minute check of the car in the pit before the big race. COURTESY BOB SHARP RACING. WILTON, CONN.

a better and more secure future waiting for you in automotive mechanics or engineering, and both are an important part of racing.

Mechanics, headed by a chief mechanic, make up the pit crew—those who work swiftly to keep the car in top running order when it stops at the pit while the race is in progress (pit stop). Of course, thorough training as a mechanic is necessary for this job.

110

Stock car races draw big crowds in communities all across the country. COURTESY ALBANY DEMOCRAT-HERALD. ALBANY, OREGON

Automotive and design engineers develop the cars. It takes people of great mechanical and engineering ability to come up with improved designs and features. So for this fine career, get as much education in the engineering field as you possibly can.

The driver, crew, and owner share in the purse that, for the winners of the big races, can be a fortune. The leaders of certain laps around the track may win lap money.

Only a few top drivers make a good living at driving alone. A handful become celebrities and gather all the extras other well-known sports figures do.

During the long climb up to the big race at Indianapolis, some drivers have companies that will sponsor them, that is, pay them a sum to help with living and other expenses. In return, the driver publicizes (endorses) the company's product, be it gasoline, tires, or whatever.

Another kind of auto racing, with stockcars, draws big

crowds, too, in large or small towns all across the country. These cars are not especially built, as are the championship cars, and little new knowledge to help the automobile industry comes out of it. The purses are not nearly as large, and though still a risky activity, the danger of death is not so ever-present.

Midget racing in very small cars that meet special requirements is popular, too. The financial investment in such a car is midget, too, which is one feature that attracts many drivers to this sport.

If racing really appeals to you, someday you might consider entering sports-car rallies. They are growing in popularity and most people enter just for the fun of it.

Figure skating

Tiny tots learning to twirl on thin silver blades may be urged to practice more and more by their parents who see in their child's future stardom with all its wealth, excitement, and glamour.

When skaters reach their teenage years, the competition for awards in many age, sex, and style categories grows more intense. The most coveted award is an Olympic medal, preferably the first-place gold.

Skating requires more practice hours a day and more individual coaching than any other winter or summer Olympic event. What does this mean to the skater and his or her family?

First of all, money . . . easily $10,000 a year. Summers at skating camps are a must. And education at private schools is often necessary so that a study schedule can be worked out that allows time for skating. Many children as young as seven are sent to live with strangers to be near

112

Figure skating requires more practice hours a day and more individual coaching than any other winter or summer Olympic event.
COURTESY DOROTHY HAMILL

their coaches. So it's easy to see that a hundred thousand dollars may be drained from the family's budget by the time the skater reaches seventeen. Yet he or she must continue practicing those long, hard hours without pay, for until the skater is holding a top amateur award, turning pro will reap no particular benefits.

Families often break up over the demands of skating— the money drain, the travel, husband and wife living apart as they often must, since most contenders are too young to travel alone.

Winners of top competition enjoy celebrity status. These lucky few may then turn pro and eventually earn a good living by skating. They often join ice shows where their glamorous but hard lives are not much different from dancers who take to the road in other shows.

Some medal winners become big stars, and that's the bait that keeps the others going. One figure-skater recently signed contracts for an ice show, television, and movies that will earn her more than two million dollars.

When age or the desire to settle down overcomes the skater, he or she often turns to teaching where the pay is good—from $8 to $20 an hour. The job market is very small but easing a bit now that many more ice-skating rinks are opening (because of the hockey boom).

Other skaters may work behind the scenes for an ice show or head for a totally different field. But many are seldom prepared for anything else because serious skaters usually don't have the time to get a good education.

Bowling

One out of five Americans bowl, making it far and away

A special effects shot of a bowler in action. COURTESY U.S. NAVY

the top sport for participation. Forty million dollars a year is spent on bowling balls alone.

Top bowlers, on tour with the Professional Bowlers

115

Association (PBA), can strike it rich now that they compete on live or recorded television shows in cities across the country. Purses have contained more than $125,000, with $25,000 going to the high scorer. And each year prize money increases as more and more people sit by their television sets and try to pick up a few pointers by watching how the pros do it.

But the pros didn't do it by sitting watching television. Years and years of practice, game after game—that's what's involved for success here. Again, only a few will be able to earn a good living in this highly competitive field.

If bowling is your favorite sport, and you're a high scorer, enter competition at your local lanes. More than 20,000 high school seniors try for top honors in regional championships. The twenty-four or so who make it win $1000 and the right to enter the annual All-American Youth Bowling Championships. These competitors from all across the country meet for two days. The top scorer, in each of four categories, receives a $1000 scholarship prize.

Some of these young people will eventually try for the PBA pro tour. A few might make it. Most will use their prize to educate or train themselves for another career and continue to enjoy bowling as a hobby.

Wrestling

Professional wrestling was once held in high regard. But promoters of the sport began to treat it as a show with actors. So pro wrestling deteriorated to the point where it must now be billed as an exhibition and is confined to the heavyweight class. Men, and a few women, wrestle using

116

Fans beg for autographs from this popular professional wrestler. As an amateur, he was a college champion, but his performance must now be billed as an exhibition. COURTESY ALBANY DEMOCRAT-HERALD. ALBANY, OREGON

outrageous names. But the public enjoys the shows so much that the best performers do several bouts a week and make over $100,000 a year.

Good wrestlers in the amateur area where it is still a highly-respected sport should stay amateurs, unless they wish to enter show business and win or lose bouts according to a show manager's will.

14 / Sports and Women

Throughout this book, we've tried to show that there are job opportunities in sports for women as well as men. Medical science has tossed aside the old belief that girls injure more easily than boys, that being "female" hinders athletic performance. (In the 1956 Olympics, three gold-medal winners were pregnant!)

In growing numbers women are moving out of the bleachers and off the cheerleaders' benches and onto the playing fields and into the arenas. They've found sponsors and television coverage that have made tennis an "equal opportunity" sport. Golf, too, has rich rewards for women, though not nearly as many as for men. Yet in most areas, "for men only" attitudes still prevail. A few examples of discrimination follow.

The major league team sports and others that have always been considered "masculine" are closed to women except for behind-the-scenes jobs. Even that's a recent breakthrough.

Girls have broken into the jockey lineup, but in spite of their impressive records, few horse owners will take a chance on a woman.

In growing numbers, women are moving into all areas of sports. COURTESY ALBANY DEMOCRAT-HERALD. ALBANY, OREGON

This young woman is one of several who competes in harness racing.
COURTESY YONKERS RACEWAY

Now that young girls are permitted to play in the Little Leagues, the course of organized baseball may change someday. But for now, women who play ball can only find spots on women's softball teams. Most of these teams are not self-supporting. Members pass the hat during the game, hoping to collect enough money to meet expenses.

121

Women have broken into the jockey lineup but in spite of their impressive records, few horseowners will take a chance on them.
COURTESY NEW YORK RACING ASSOCIATION

But some teams have managed to get publicity, find companies to sponsor them, and build a small but wildly-enthusiastic following.

But this is another gripe that women have. Television, which creates the publicity that brings in the money at the box-office and builds superstars, pays little attention to women in professional sports. In 1973, one network devoted 365 sports hours to men and one hour to women. Another network spent only 10 of its 260 sports hours on women's events. But this, too, is changing though women

Women in tennis have found sponsors and television coverage and have fought long and hard for "equal opportunities" in the sport.
COURTESY VIRGINIA SLIMS CIRCUIT

are still banned from some of the press boxes, especially in the smaller towns.

A look at the future

Athletic budgets in some school districts still allot only one dollar for girls' sports for every $250 spent for boys'. Fifty thousand men are awarded athletic college scholarships each year, and only about one hundred women.

But a change is in the making at the school level where it can have the most effect. School systems are beginning to understand that girl students should have the same right as boys to enjoy all the benefits of a vigorous sports program. Most experts believe that as a result, the boys will come to accept the girls as worthy athletes, teammates, and opponents. This attitude is bound to carry into adulthood. Eventually it could result in the equality in sports that women are determined to gain.

Index